The  of God

The Revelation of the Merciful Presence of God

by
Canon Michael Lewis

All booklets are published thanks to the generous support of the members of the Catholic Truth Society

CATHOLIC TRUTH SOCIETY
PUBLISHERS TO THE HOLY SEE

Contents

To Make Known the Name of the Father............3

What's in a Name? 5

The Burning Bush................................9

I Am Who I Am 11

The Name and the Divine Mercy..................15

The Mystery of the Name 17

The Giving of the Name.........................23

YHWH and Yeshua 26

The Words of the Lord on his Name..............32

The Name that is Above All Other Names.........40

On the Invocation of the Name 47

Endnotes......................................54

All rights reserved. First published 2014 by The Incorporated Catholic Truth Society, 40-46 Harleyford Road London SE11 5AY Tel: 020 7640 0042 Fax: 020 7640 0046. © 2014 The Incorporated Catholic Truth Society. All biblical references are from the Revised Standard Version Catholic Edition.

ISBN 978 1 86082 896 6

To Make Known the Name of the Father

Just before he left the Upper Room with his disciples to cross over the Kidron Valley to go to the garden of Gethsemane, our Lord prayed to his Father: "I made known to them your name, and I will make it known, that the love with which thou hast loved me may be in them, and I in them." (*Jn* 17:26)

Here, Christ prays to his Father, declaring the whole purpose of his ministry, so soon to climax in his passion, death and resurrection. He came to make known the name of the Father and, in so doing, to make it possible for us to share in the very life of the most holy Trinity and become partakers of the divine nature.

If we ourselves were asked to describe the purpose of Christ's mission, we would not answer in terms of making known the name of the Father. We would probably say that Christ came to do the will of his Father and to save us from our sins - both of which replies, of course, would be included in the all-encompassing theme of the glorification of the Name. Clearly, Christ's words must mean more than is immediately apparent to our twenty-first century minds. What then do his words mean for us? Why is the divine Name so important?

Even the most cursory reading of the sacred text will show that the name of the Lord is one of the major themes in Scripture. The Psalms alone contain over one hundred references to the name of the Lord. The problem is, however, that precisely because these references are so ubiquitous, we can without thinking fail to appreciate their full significance. The sheer abundance of such references can easily lead us to regard them almost as if they were a part of the biblical furniture, something whose full significance is hidden because it is in plain sight.

The best commentary on the New Testament is the Old. The Second Vatican Council taught the "the study of the sacred page should be the very soul of sacred theology" (*Dei Verbum*, ¶24). This booklet seeks to show why Christ saw his mission in terms of making known the name of his Father. We shall explore the reasons why the mystery of the name of God is such a key leitmotif in the wonderful symphony of Scripture. If we attune our ear, then we shall the better appreciate something of the great harmony of the sacred text and the better understand why our Lord should have spoken of his mission in such luminous and comforting words.

What's in a Name?

About 3300 or so years ago, in the burning bush on Mount Sinai, God revealed his Name to Moses, a revelation that in the words of the *Catechism of the Catholic Church* proved "to be the fundamental one for both the Old and the New covenants."[1] This revelation was fundamental because it was the foundation of all that was to follow. Indeed, the whole story of redemption is essentially the story of how by word and by deed God is true to his name.

What began with the revelation of the Name in the Sinai wilderness became visible in the stable at Bethlehem with the birth of the incarnate Word. As Pope Benedict XVI wrote:

> "Concealed within the name of Jesus is the tetragrammaton, the mysterious name from Mount Horeb, here expanded into the statement: Jesus saves. The, as it were, "incomplete" name from Sinai is finally spoken. The God who is, the saving God, now present. The revelation of God's name, which began in the burning bush, comes to completion in Jesus (cf. *Jn* 17:26)."[2]

The question arises as to why the revelation of a name should be such a pivotal event in the history of salvation. After all, many people see names as little more than mere labels, arbitrary things formed by the accident of culture and language. With Shakespeare's Juliet, the modern person will say:

> "What's in a name? That which we call a rose
> By any other name would smell as sweet."

If she had asked her question in biblical times, Juliet would probably have received the reply, "you are." In the Hebrew mind, name and the person were one: "as his name is, so is he." (*1 S* 25:25)

Far from being a mere label, the name was seen as a manifestation of the person named, a part of them, a potent symbol that not only expressed but, in a mysterious way, was something actually charged with and expressing the being and the underlying reality of the person named. Names reveal the attributes of the person. This is why in Genesis, for example, whenever a man is born or given a given a new name, the meaning of that name is explained. If the names of mortal beings matter so much, how much more does the name of God?

The Scriptures see a man's soul as present in his name, and thus to reveal one's name is to reveal oneself. Names are analogous to a sacrament: they make the person present. This is why a person can sometimes be reluctant to disclose his name to an enquirer, as with Manoah and the angel of the Lord: "And Manoah said to the angel of the Lord, 'What is your name, so that, when your words come true, we may honour you?' And the angel of the Lord said to him, 'Why do you ask my name, seeing it is wonderful?'" (*Jg* 13:17-18)

The underlying thought here is that to know a person's name is to acquire a certain power over them. To disclose one's name is to make oneself vulnerable.

The *Catechism of the Catholic Church* summarises the whole semitic theology of the Name thus:

> "God revealed himself to his people Israel by making his Name known to them. A name expresses a person's essence and identity, and the meaning of this person's life. God has a name; he is not an anonymous force. To disclose one's name is to make oneself known to others; in a way it is to hand oneself over by becoming accessible, capable of being known more intimately and addressed personally." (*CCC*, ¶203)

So when Moses asked the name of God, he was asking for much more than that God simply identify himself. God does not have a name as you and I have a personal name. Moreover, Moses was running a real danger of attempting to reduce God to the level of one deity among many others such as Baal, Zeus or Ra. God is not one god among many who needs to be distinguished by name: God simply is and the rest are not beings at all. So God's reply to Moses is both an answer and a non-answer.

With profound insight, Pope Benedict XVI wrote that the prohibition on the uttering of the Name that emerged in later Judaism sprang ultimately from a recognition that the Name revealed to Moses can never be reduced to the level of being one name among many. He commented that the Israelites were:

> "therefore perfectly right on refusing to utter this self-designation of God expressed in the word YHWH, so as to avoid degrading it to the level of names of pagan deities. By the same token, recent Bible translations were wrong to write out this name - which Israel always regarded as mysterious and unutterable - as if it were just any old name. By doing so, they have dragged the mystery of God, which cannot be captured in images or in names lips can utter, down to the level of some familiar item within a common history of religions."[3]

Soon after the Pope wrote these words, the Vatican's Congregation for Divine Worship and the Sacraments issued an instruction prohibiting the use, singing or pronunciation of the name of God as 'YHWH' with the insertion of the letter 'a' between the first two consonants and the letter 'e' between the last two consonants at Mass and in all other liturgical celebrations. Following Christian tradition since time immemorial, Catholics are instructed to use the title 'Lord' in Catholic translations of the Scriptures whenever 'YHWH' appears in the Hebrew text. In accordance with this and Pope Benedict's own practice, this booklet uses the four-letter name 'YHWH' without the addition of these two vowels.

The Burning Bush

Tending the flock of his father-in-law Jethro in the Sinai wilderness, Moses led the sheep to Horeb, the mountain of God. Out of the midst of a burning thorn bush, the angel of the Lord appeared to Moses in a flame of fire that did not consume the bush. Moses turned aside to see this wonder and God, seeing him turn aside, called him twice by name. Moses's reply to God's call is simply to say, "Here I am." This is the only response that a man can make in the presence of the Holy, the response of a child to the summons of a parent, of the 'I' responding to the 'Thou' of the God who calls him urgently by name.

God warned Moses not to approach too close and told him to remove his shoes for he is standing on holy ground. This sense of the numinous is an essential part of the theophany, for what is man before God? Moses hides his face for he is afraid to look on God. Then the great revelation of the Name begins as God promises salvation for captive Israel but first he reveals himself to Moses as the God of his own father Amram and of the Patriarchs:

"When the Lord saw that he turned aside to see, God called to him out of the bush, 'Moses, Moses!' And he said, 'Here am I.' Then he said, 'Do not come near; put off your shoes from your feet, for the place on which

> you are standing is holy ground.' And he said, 'I am the God of your father, the God of Abraham, the God of Isaac, and the God of Jacob.' And Moses hid his face, for he was afraid to look at God." (*Ex* 3:4-6)

Perhaps because our attention is so focused on the name to be revealed, we can overlook the full significance of the bush. The burning bush is a visual symbol of the answer that God will give to Moses when Moses asks him to name himself. The bush that burns without being consumed is a sign that points to the otherness, the sheer transcendence and mystery of the God who alone exists of himself. A flame that burns by itself without fuel is something that is not to be found anywhere in nature. Just as the flame burns of itself without any created source, so too with God: he is radically other than creation and alone exists necessarily. God derives his being from no other.

Some may object that to interpret the bush in this way is to impose a philosophical category of thought alien to Hebrew text, but the whole point of the bush is that it is not consumed by the flames: the flames derive their energy and vitality from nothing in this world. That was what caught Moses's attention in the first place. The philosophical interpretation is certainly contained in the full meaning of the text and is consistent with the narrative. God alone exists of himself; he is the God who has covenanted with Abraham and yet is utterly transcendent and infinitely strong to save.

I Am Who I Am

This Lord is not the Absolute of the philosophers, an unknown God, but the God of human beings, of great and small alike. He is the God of the obscure Amram, Moses's father, who is not even named here and whose name appears only twice in the whole of Scripture. God reveals himself as the God who has covenanted himself with Abraham, the God of Isaac and Jacob, the God of the promises who will never abandon his people.

Moses therefore asks God his name:

"Then Moses said to God, 'If I come to the people of Israel and say to them, "The God of your fathers has sent me to you," and they ask me, "What is his name?" what shall I say to them?' God said to Moses, 'I am who I am.' [*Ehyeh Asher Ehyeh*] And he said, 'Say this to the people of Israel, "I am has sent me to you."' God also said to Moses, 'Say this to the people of Israel, "The Lord [YHWH], the God of your fathers, the God of Abraham, the God of Isaac, and the God of Jacob, has sent me to you": this is my name for ever, and thus I am to be remembered throughout all generations.'" (*Ex* 3:13-16)

Above all, the Lord is the God who speaks to man, addresses him by word. In man's past, he is the God of Amram, Abraham, Isaac and Jacob. In man's present, he is the God who tells Moses that he has seen the misery and affliction of his people in bondage in Egypt. Now he has come down to deliver them out of the hands of the Egyptians. In man's future, he is the God who will bring the people of Israel out of Egypt "to a very broad land, a land flowing with milk and honey."

This same God of the Patriarchs will be with Moses who is now to be his chosen instrument to free his people Israel. God names himself as the God who is, who was and will be with his people. In thus revealing his Name, his intimate nature, to Moses, God is revealing his mercy for his people.

Moses had gone to the holy mountain as a shepherd and there he encountered the true shepherd of Israel, the Lord himself who will lead his flock out of slavery to the Promised Land.

The divine name

The divine Name has two forms. The first – *'Ehyeh'* ('I Am') - is used when God himself is speaking. *Ehyeh* is the Qal imperfect, first person singular, of the root *hayah*, 'to be'. When others speak of God, the third person masculine singular form is used from the same root, that is 'He Is' or 'He Who Is.' Both forms are derived from the same root. The first person singular can also be translated as 'I will be what I will be,' and this was the translation favoured by Rashi, the greatest of all Jewish commentators. The verb has an active quality about it: in our past, present and future, God is always totally 'I Am.'

The name of YHWH appears 6828 times in the Hebrew Scriptures. The precise interpretation of the four root consonants of the name YHWH has been a matter for intense speculation and has generated a vast and extensive literature. This name has become known as the tetragrammaton from the Greek *tettara* (four) and *gramma* (letter). Some scholars have interpreted the name in a causative sense, as "the one who causes to be." The Jewish Greek translation of the Old Testament, the Septuagint, gives "I am the one who is." God's name defines his essence. As such, the name cannot be revealed: God both reveals and hides his name; yet, paradoxically, God's answer to Moses will be sufficient to satisfy the questions of the Israelites when they ask him who has sent him. The sense is conveyed that God will actively manifest himself to his people: "I will be what I will be." In the future, the eternal God will manifest his everlasting love for his people by being with them to save and redeem them.

For Pope Benedict XVI, the central issue is not the enigmatic nature of God's reply but the fact that "this God designates himself simply as the 'I am.' He just is without any qualification. And that also means, of course, that he is always there - for human beings, yesterday, today, and tomorrow."[4]

The name of YHWH is not a name in the ordinary sense of the word. Normally names have the effect of making something a mental object. We use names to comprehend the world around us, to distinguish objects and set them in a context. God can indeed be the object of our thought, but our minds cannot comprehend him nor can he be reduced to the level of an object among other objects.

The tetragrammaton truly evokes the reality of God himself. To quote again from the *Catechism*:

> "The revelation of the ineffable name 'I Am Who Am' contains then the truth that God alone IS. The Greek Septuagint translation of the Hebrew Scriptures, and following it the Church's Tradition, understood the divine name in this sense: God is the fullness of being and of every perfection, without origin and without end. All creatures receive all that they are and have from him; but he alone is his very being, and he is of himself everything that he is." (CCC, ❡213)

The Name of the four letters - *Yod-Heh-Vav-Heh* - is the distinctive name in the Old Testament, expressing both God's eternity and his loving-kindness and mercy.

The Name and the Divine Mercy

God's response to Moses is an existential answer, an answer that comes out of the heart of the divine fire of God's love itself. The "I am" of the Lord echoes the "Here I am" of Moses. At the burning bush, God reveals his Name in the first person. He is there with Moses; he is here now as he was with Abraham, Isaac and Jacob, and as he will be with his people in the future. God names himself by saying he has been, is now and will be with his people. All tenses are present in the Name because time past and time future are all embraced in God's eternal now. For the very first time, God calls Israel, "my people."

We see the divine mercy and tenderness in the revelation of the Name. The medieval Jewish commentator Rashi noted that the vision was in the very heart (Hebrew *lev*) of the burning bush. The divine compassion is shown by the choice of a humble thorn bush and not another tree. God suffers with Israel and hence appears not in some mighty cedar but in the lowliest plant.

In Exodus 34, we have the second proclamation of the name to Moses at Sinai:

"And the Lord descended in the cloud and stood with him there, and proclaimed the name of the Lord. The Lord passed before him, and proclaimed, "The Lord, the Lord, a God merciful and gracious, slow to anger, and abounding in steadfast love and faithfulness". (*Ex* 34:5-6)

In this remarkable passage, God proclaims his own attributes and the first of these is mercy, the divine compassion.

The Name revealed to Moses from the heart of the burning bush is the name of the One who will hang on the cross crowned with thorns. The promise to Moses had been that YHWH would be with his people. Jesus is YHWH with us. YHWH-with-us is Jesus. In Christian iconography, the cross inside the nimbus that surrounds the head of Christ is normally inscribed on the three visible arms with the three Greek letters *omicron*, *omega* and *nu*, which mean "He who is." In Jesus, that promise made to Moses is fulfilled for all ages and for all men.

The name of YHWH, the tetragrammaton, lies beyond man's understanding and yet it is the revelation of God, of his merciful presence. Israel's religious quest is to seek the face of the Lord and to hear his Name. When the time had been fully prepared, God was to reveal his face and manifest his Name in the most wonderful way of all, by the incarnation. Then, unasked, the angel would reveal the Name by which alone we can be saved.

The Mystery of the Name

The enigmatic and mysterious nature of the name of YHWH extends even to the way in which it should be pronounced. Hebrew does not have letters for vowels as such. Out of their profound reverence for the name of God, the Jews normally substituted the title *Adonai* ('my Lord') whenever the tetragrammaton occurred in the text. As Emmanuel Levinas, the Jewish philosopher, commented, "The name *Adonai* - which, in its turn, must not be pronounced in vain - is the name of the tetragrammaton. The name has a name!"[5] Many centuries later, the Massoretes added vowel signs above and below the sacred consonantal text to facilitate their pronunciation and standardise the oral tradition. However, whenever the word 'YHWH' was written, they used the vowel markings of the substituted title *Adonai* as a sign that this title was to be read in its place whenever the Name appeared in the sacred text. Christian misunderstanding of this practice led to the vowel signs of *Adonai* being inserted into the consonants of 'YHWH' and the incorrect neologism 'JeHoVaH' began to appear in some Christian translations of the Hebrew Bible.

The Talmudic prohibition on pronouncing the name of God relates strictly speaking only to the four-letter Name but, outside of prayer and study, a Jew will avoid pronouncing even the other names of God. '*Adonai*' will be used in prayer but in everyday speech and writing God will be referred to simply as '*ha-Shem*' ('the Name') or some other form such as '*Adoshem*' (the first part of '*Adonai*' plus '*Shem*').

In the Greek translation of the Old Testament, the Septuagint, '*Kyrios*' ('Lord') is used in place of 'YHWH', a practice followed by most English translations.

The *Catechism* comments thus on the Greek version of the divine Name as 'He Who Is':

> "God is 'He Who Is', from everlasting to everlasting, and as such remains ever faithful to himself and to his promises. The revelation of the ineffable name 'I Am Who Am' contains then the truth that God alone IS. The Greek Septuagint translation of the Hebrew Scriptures, and following it the Church's Tradition, understood the divine name in this sense: God is the fullness of being and of every perfection, without origin and without end. All creatures receive all that they are and have from him; but he alone is his very being, and he is of himself everything that he is." (*CCC*, ¶212-213)

T

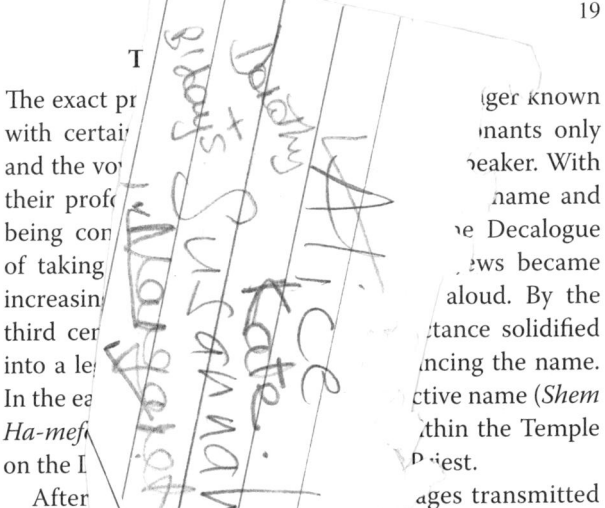

The exact pr..iger known
with certai...nants only
and the vo...eaker. With
their profo..name and
being con...e Decalogue
of taking...ews became
increasin...aloud. By the
third cer...tance solidified
into a le...ncing the name.
In the ea...ctive name (*Shem
Ha-mef*..thin the Temple
on the L...Priest.

After ....ages transmitted
the original pronunciation to a select band of their
disciples once every seventh year, but this practice
eventually ceased. In his Antiquities, Josephus wrote
that it was unlawful to say the Name.[6] The Talmud
forbade the saying of the Name aloud, and gradually
the original pronunciation was lost.

The well-known form of YHWH with the insertion of
'a' and 'e' (now prohibited in Catholic liturgical use and
Catholic translations of the Scriptures) represents modern
scholarship's best attempt at recreating the original
vocalisation. It comes from certain texts found in certain of
the early Church Fathers, especially from a fourth-century
reference by Theodoret of Cyprus, giving the Samaritan

version. But, at best, it is only an approximation and it is by no means established beyond all doubt.

The name and God's presence

What is certain is that the theme of the Name runs like a golden thread throughout the Old Testament. God's divine power and glory are constantly seen as present and active in his Name. The angel in whom God has set his Name leads Israel through the desert to the Promised Land. Closely related to this idea is that of the Shekinah, the protective and tabernacling presence of YHWH with his people.

The word Shekinah comes from the word *shakhan*, 'to dwell', and refers to the presence or indwelling of God in a certain place. Although the term is used explicitly only after the Old Testament, it describes an important motif in the Hebrew Bible, especially in the Deuteronomic writings where the Shekinah is very closely linked to the theme of the Name.

This theology of the name enabled the inspired writers to convey the idea of a 'localised' presence of the God who transcends the created order. Although YHWH dwells in heaven, he chooses a place in which to cause his Name to dwell (*Dt* 14:23,16:6 and 14:24). Dwelling in the temple, the Name of YHWH is the manifestation and the sign of his immanent presence with Israel, of his protection and covenant love, his *hesed*.

There is a growing tendency in the Old Testament to treat the Name almost as if it were a person in its own right. Isaiah looks forward to the coming of the Name, for where the Name is, there is YHWH, approaching in majesty to save his people:

> "Behold, the name of the Lord comes from far,
> burning with his anger,
> and in thick rising smoke;
> his lips are full of indignation,
> and his tongue is like a devouring fire" (*Is* 30:27)

The Psalms are full of references to the name of the Lord:

> "Save me, O God, by thy name,
> and vindicate me by thy might.
> With a freewill offering I will sacrifice to thee;
> I will give thanks to thy name, O Lord, for it is good."
> (*Ps* 54:1,6)

Always the Lord is "true to his name," and the Psalmists find in that Name their joy, their hope, their exultation, their refuge and their salvation. When the priests bless the people, they 'put' the name on the Israelites:

> "'The Lord bless you and keep you:
> The Lord make his face to shine upon you, and be gracious to you:
> The Lord lift up his countenance upon you, and give you peace.'
>
> "So shall they put my name upon the people of Israel, and I will bless them." (*Nb* 6:24-27)

Micah pictures the Messianic age as an eternal walking in the name of Lord. The coming of the kingdom and the hallowing of the Name are bound together. Israel's whole mission and vocation is to walk eternally in the name of YHWH: "For all the peoples walk, each in the name of its god, but we will walk in the name of the Lord our God for ever and ever." (*Mi* 4:5)

Zechariah's prophecy of the Messianic age contains a text of key importance:

"And the Lord will become king over all the earth; on that day the Lord will be one and his name one." (*Zc* 14:9)

Kingdom and Name were always seen as intertwined as in the second line of the Shema, the most important of all Jewish prayers: "Blessed be the name of his glorious kingdom for ever and ever."

Rabbinic thought came to associate the name of the Lord with God's special relationship with his people Israel, in contrast with the more generic name of Elohim, which denotes God in his universal aspect. In their mystical writings, the Kabbalists taught that the name of YHWH represented the divine Rahamim, the compassion of God, which mediates between his *hesed*, his merciful love, and his *gevurah* or *din*, his stern justice. Rabbi Jonathan Sacks expressed it succinctly: "The tetragrammaton refers to God as we encounter him in intimacy, compassion and love."[7]

The Giving of the Name

Although Joseph is not the biological father of the Messiah, Matthew establishes carefully the legal paternity of Joseph according to Jewish law. Normally, a Jewish father would choose the name of his son according to family tradition and custom, but here the angel tells Joseph what the name of the Virgin's son is to be. The naming of the Messiah is a sign of the divine paternity. Since the role of an angel is to bring a message from God, it is God who has chosen the name of the Messiah and of his Son. Now what is eternal begins to exist in time, and the name of the Word made flesh, eternally pre-existent in the mind of God, is now made known on earth.

There are all sorts of rich biblical echoes here. God is at work in Mary. She is indeed the gate of heaven, for in her womb she carries the Son of the Most High. She is truly *Beth-el*, the house of God. Just as the bush was aflame with the divine glory and was not consumed, so Mary carries the Word in her womb while remaining ever a virgin. Just as his namesake went down to Egypt, so Joseph takes the Holy Family down to exile in Egypt. This is to fulfil what was written, that God would call his son out of Egypt.

Christ is the new Israel. In Exodus 4:22, Israel is called God's 'firstborn son' and the first revelation of the name on the eve of the Exodus is echoed in the revelation of the name of Jesus. The name the people will call Jesus is 'Immanuel', which means 'God-with-us'.

One subtlety in the Greek original that is lost in some English translations is the angelic instruction to name the child 'Jesus'. The Greek actually says, "you…will call his name Jesus," not "you will name him Jesus." It is to be noted that the great stress is given to the name of the child for as the name is, so is he. Similarly, the Greek of Matthew 1:23 reads literally "and they will call the name of him 'Immanuel' which means 'God with us.'" For all time, God will be with his people. In the Christ child, the Name is present among us: Lord, Saviour and God with us.

The Shekinah had been present in the burning bush and is now present in the Blessed Virgin. In Rabbinic tradition, the cloud of the Tabernacle in Exodus 40:34-38 was the cloud of the Shekinah. Mary is 'overshadowed' by the Holy Spirit and becomes the place of the Shekinah, the new Ark of the Covenant, the dwelling-place for the Name.

In her song, she praises the name of the Lord for "the Mighty One has done great things for me, and holy is his name." Mary's reaction is the spontaneous one to proclaim the holiness of God's name. The Lord, YHWH, is with Mary. She is the dwelling-place of the Name, the new Ark of the Covenant.

Before the moment when the incarnation took place in time, Gabriel revealed to Mary the Name that from all eternity has existed in the mind of God, the name of God with us, and God with us is Jesus.

After eight days had passed from the birth of the Messiah, the time came to circumcise the child. Obedient to God's word, Mary and Joseph call him Jesus, the name given by the angel before he was conceived in the womb. He becomes a child of the covenant and henceforth bears this Name which sums up all he is and all he will do. There is nothing arbitrary here; nothing is left to chance.

With the coming of the Messiah, the promise of the divine mercy contained in the revelation of the divine mercy in the name of YHWH finds its fulfilment. The King has come into his own and the long exile of the world is over, for the time of restoration has begun.

God's name is One, but from now on it can never be the name of a stranger, beyond the lips of man, known only to a select group of initiates and to be uttered once a year by the High Priest in the temple on Yom Kippur. The name is on our lips, in our mind and in our heart. If we confess with our mouth that Jesus is Lord and believe in our heart that God raised Him from the dead, we shall be saved.

YHWH and Yeshua

Whenever God gives a name to a man or a woman in Scripture, that name expresses their mission and their being. The Greek *Iesous* represents the Hebrew and Aramaic 'Yeshua', and is usually translated as 'YHWH saves' or 'YHWH is salvation'. The Hebrew for 'He will save' is *yoshia*, and comes from the same root as Yeshua. 'Yeshua' is simply the abbreviated form of the Hebrew 'Yehoshua' (Joshua), a shortened form that became common in the period after the return from exile in Babylon.

We know from the Septuagint, the Greek translation of the Hebrew Scriptures, and from the first century Jewish historian Josephus that Yeshua was a common name in the time of Christ, but strictly speaking it is a name that can only truly be proper to Mary's son who alone is the true Jesus for 'He will save his people from their sins'. In other words, the very name of Jesus declares his mission: Jesus comes to us in order to be our Jesus.

The Scriptures give us a definition of the name of Joshua from which the name of Yeshua stems:

"Joshua the son of Nun was mighty in war, and was the successor of Moses in prophesying. He became, in accordance with his name, a great saviour of God's elect, to take vengeance on the enemies that rose against them." (*Si* 46:1)

Moses gave the name Joshua ('YHWH saves') to Hoshea ('saviour' or 'deliverer'), to stress that it would be the Lord himself who would save his people. Joshua himself is not the saviour: it is the Lord himself who alone can save his people. His name is not absolute but provisional, pointing to the true Joshua. Jesus receives the name of Jesus because he will save the people from their sins. What is foreshadowed in Joshua is fulfilled in a transcendent manner in Jesus who is the Saviour, the one who overcomes Satan and wins an eternal inheritance for God's people. Jesus does not lead Israel across a physical river into a physical land. By being baptised by John in the river Jordan, Christ sanctifies the whole of creation. By his death and resurrection, he leads us through the waters of baptism into the Promised Land and to share in the very life of God himself.

Nothing is left to chance. It is highly significant that the Archangel Gabriel revealed the name of Jesus to Mary before the conception of the child. In Rabbinic tradition, the name of the Messiah was one of the things that existed before the creation of the cosmos: the coming of the Messiah was a part of God's original plan, programmed into the very act of creation itself.

The name that all can invoke

The sacred humanity is bone of our bone, and flesh of our flesh. YHWH is with his people in the most intimate way of all: the heavens are rent open and God has come down among us. The ineffable name of YHWH is made visible in Jesus and all can now invoke the name that could not be uttered. Just as man longs to see God, so he longs to know his name.

Man's response to God's word is faith, faith in the mystery of the incarnation and redemption. When the Christian calls on the name of Jesus with faith, the invocation is an entering into the mystery of the Pasch of Christ, because we could not call him unless he first called us. The mystery of the divine mercy is made present. Our hearts are opened to the rays of love radiating from his pierced side.

With this in mind, we begin to realise something of the force of such texts as the following:

"In that day you will ask nothing of me. Truly, truly, I say to you, if you ask anything of the Father, he will give it to you in my name." (*Jn* 16:23)

"And there is salvation in no-one else, for there is no other name under heaven given among men by which we must be saved." (*Ac* 4:12)

It is not by accident that the name of Jesus should be both the first and the last name to appear in the New Testament. Matthew's Gospel begins with the origins of "Jesus Christ, the son of David, the son of Abraham" and the Apocalypse ends with the fervent prayer that Jesus may come and for his grace to be with all the saints. Symbolically, the name of Jesus contains and frames the whole of the good news of the Kingdom of God.

The Lord, who holds creation in the palm of his hand, tells us his name. His name reveals that he is and will be with us, the Saviour, the compassionate one, the one who was, who is and will be, YHWH.

God's love for his people stops at nothing. His gift to us is himself and his love has no limits or boundaries. The Father sends his Son who makes known to us all the mysteries contained in his name, the infinite compassion in his heart for man. When Philip asked to see the Father, our Lord answered by saying that to have seen him was to have seen the Father. So it is with the name of YHWH. To know Jesus is to know He who is.

The five-letter name

In the New Covenant, the continuation and fulfilment of the Old, the pentagrammaton, the five-letter name, is revealed - the name of Jesus, which in Hebrew and Aramaic is 'Yeshua'. Now, the name can be pronounced.

The five sacred letters of the name can be vocalised. Just as the Word is made flesh and becomes visible, so too the name can now not only be uttered, but can be invoked by all, for in Jesus dwells all the fullness of the divinity.

In the sixteenth century, several Christian writers were either consciously or unconsciously influenced by the thought and imagery of the Kabbalah, the Jewish mystical tradition. Perhaps the most notable of these was Luis de Leon (1527-1591) whose book *The Names of Christ* is one of the great masterpieces of the golden age of Spanish literature. Partially of Jewish descent on his mother's side, he wrote these beautiful words on the spiritual relationship between the tetragrammaton and the name of our Lord in Hebrew:

> "One aspect seems important to me. The Hebrew word for Jesus is 'Yehoshuah'.... And in it we find all the letters that go into the name of God in Hebrew, the so-called 'four-letter name of God' or 'tetragrammaton,' plus two letters more. As you know, the name of God with four letters is a name that cannot be uttered, because vowels are not pronounced, because we do not know what their real sound should be, or because of the respect due to God, or else, as I have suspected sometimes, because it is like the mumbling sounds that a dumb person utters as an expression of friendship, affection, love: without a clear pattern,

shapeless, as if God wanted us men to use a word to express his infinite being, a clumsy word or a sound that would make us understand that God is too large to be embraced or expressed in any clear way by our understanding and our tongue. Pronouncing such a name is tantamount to admitting that we are limited and dumb when we come face to face with God. Our confusion and our mumbling are a hymn of praise, as David declared; the name of God is ineffable and unutterable. And yet in Jesus' name two letters have been added and the name can indeed be pronounced and said out loud with a clear meaning. What happened with Christ also happened with Christ's name: It is the clear portrait of God. In Christ we see God joined to a man's soul and body. God's name, which could not be said, now has two more letters and it can be said, mysteries can be revealed, made visible, can be talked about. Christ is Jesus, that is to say, a combination of God and man, of a name that cannot be uttered and a name that can."[8]

The Words of the Lord on his Name

What our Lord himself says about his name must lie at the very heart of our meditation on the mystery of the name. Christ speaks to us in the whole of Scripture, but there is a particular intensity in his own words as recorded by the Evangelists. In the Gospels, in the most wonderful and sublime fashion, the Word addresses each one of us directly and personally.

It is immediately apparent that Christ sees the concepts of name, person and self as inextricably linked. He speaks of his name in terms of its being charged with his presence and power, the symbol of who and what he is. The name is the person manifest and expressed. It would have been surprising if our Lord as a Jew had thought otherwise.

When we collate what our Lord says about his own name, we see that he is speaks in a totally semitic way of his name as a way of referring to actions done in his person, on his behalf or by his authority. In his name, prophecies are made, demons exorcised and mighty deeds worked. He warns against false Messiahs who will come claiming his authority and who will use his name fraudulently. To receive a child in his name is to receive him. The disciple will be hated because of his name.

In his name, the Gentiles will hope and repentance will be preached to all the nations. Those who give up everything for the sake of the name will inherit eternal life. The Messiah comes "in the name of the Lord," and the Messianic cry of the people Hosanna ('save us') is addressed to him whose very name means salvation. From what our Lord says of his own name, it is clear that it has a transcendent power and dignity.

One saying in particular has often been quoted: "For where two or three are gathered in my name, there am I in the midst of them." (*Mt* 18:20). The full import of the saying becomes evident when we compare it to the following passage from the Talmud:

"If two sit together and words of Torah pass between them, the Shekinah abides between them, as it is said, 'Those who feared Adonai spoke together, and Adonai paid heed and listened, and a record was written before him for those who feared Adonai and thought on his name.'" (*Avot* 3:2)

Jesus and 'I Am'

Our Lord's most revolutionary and amazing words on the divine name are to be found in his self-designation as 'I Am' in the 'I Am' sayings in the fourth Gospel. The evangelist stated that his purpose in writing the Gospel was that we "may believe that Jesus is the Christ, the Son of God, and that by believing you may have life in his name." (*Jn* 20:30)

We remember, of course, that 'I am', in Greek *ego eimi*, is the Greek translation of the Hebrew *ehyeh*, the name revealed in the burning bush. Any Jew hearing someone applying this name to himself would have been totally shocked at what would have seemed the grossest blasphemy. Such a person was claiming divine status and was either mad, bad or God.

When we come to examine our Lord's use of 'I am', we find that it falls into two main groups.

The first group uses the 'I am', with a predicate nominative, that is, a noun or pronoun which follows the verb and describes the subject. Thus Christ says "I am":

1. the bread of life,
2. the door for the sheep,
3. the good shepherd,
4. the resurrection and the life,
5. the way, the truth and the life,
6. the true vine.

The second group of sayings uses 'I Am' in an absolute sense in which he makes the 'I Am', the divine name, his own:

1. "I told you that you would die in your sins, for you will die in your sins unless you believe that I am he." (*Jn* 8:24) The original Greek does not contain the pronoun "he."

2. "So Jesus said, 'When you have lifted up the Son of man, then you will know that I am he, and that I do nothing on my own authority but speak thus as the Father taught me.'" (*Jn* 8:28) Again, the original Greek does not contain the pronoun "he."

3. "Jesus said to them, 'Truly, truly, I say to you, before Abraham was, I am.' So they took up stones to throw at him; but Jesus hid himself, and went out of the temple." (*Jn* 8:58) Here, the word *genesthai* used for Abraham has the sense of 'became' or 'came into being' as contrasted with the eternal existence of the one who alone can say, "I AM."

4. St John's Gospel makes it abundantly clear that Christ saw himself as the same 'I Am' who had spoken to Moses on Mount Sinai. The revelation made to Moses was a revelation of the Word: it was the Son of God who spoke to Moses out of the burning bush, just as the glory of YHWH that Isaiah had seen in the temple had been a vision of Christ (cf. *Jn* 12:41). The God who had promised Moses that he would be with and for his people, now, and in the future as he had been in past, is the 'I am' who is one with Jesus.

In the fourth Gospel, a new basis for prayer is announced, prayer in the name of the Son. What is meant here is more than a new formula to be tagged at the end of a prayer. This teaching on "asking in his name" is inseparable from the promised gift of the Spirit, the Comforter and Consoler, the abiding presence of Jesus with those who call upon his name.

Christ has revealed and will reveal the name of the Father to the disciples so that the love with which the Father has loved him may be in them. Again and again, Christ shows us the saving power of his name and gives us the consoling certitude that our prayer in his name will be heard:

> "Whatever you ask in my name, I will do it, that the Father may be glorified in the Son; if you ask anything in my name, I will do it." (*Jn* 14:13-14)

> "You did not choose me, but I chose you and appointed you that you should go and bear fruit and that your fruit should abide; so that whatever you ask the Father in my name, he may give it to you." (*Jn* 15:16)

> "In that day you will ask nothing of me. Truly, truly, I say to you, if you ask anything of the Father, he will give it to you in my name. Hitherto you have asked nothing in my name; ask, and you will receive, that your joy may be full." (*Jn* 16:23-24)

To pray in the name of Jesus is to pray through, with and in Jesus. On Yom Kippur, the Day of the Atonement, the High Priest would enter the Holy of Holies within the temple. There he would utter the name of YHWH and offer blood sacrifice to cover the sins of the people. The people would respond with the words "Blessed be the name of his glorious kingdom, for ever and ever." Now the veil has been broken; Christ has entered once and for all into heaven and has received the name that is above all other names; every tongue confesses that Jesus Christ is Lord.

Strangely warmed

To call Jesus 'Lord' and to call on his name in prayer became a natural act of adoration. Thomas's words to our Lord, "My Lord and my God," evoke that sense of loving awe and wonder in the presence of the risen Lord which is characteristic of lived Christianity: it is not by chance that these words will often be prayed by the Christian receiving the Eucharist. What had been said of the Father in the Old Testament is extended to the Son in the New: Jesus is Lord. The Lord now has a human name, Jesus, and, as is the experience of all those who love, the name of the beloved is loved in itself and a name that is sweet to the believer's ear.

John Wesley wrote of his conversion that he felt that his heart was "strangely warmed." A sense of being "strangely warmed" by the name of Jesus has been a hallmark of Christian spirituality from the beginning and a sense that is ultimately rooted in what our Lord himself says about his own Name.

An eighteenth century hymn written by the German Pietist Gerhard Tersteegen captures something of that tender awe at the holy name:

> "Name of Jesus! highest Name!
> Name that earth and Heaven adore!
> From the heart of God it came,
> Leads me to God's heart once more."

Our way back to God's heart is an act of the divine mercy. If we cleave to God in love, he will deliver and protect us because we know his name. When we call to him, he will answer us. (cf. *Ps* 91:14-5) What comfort there is in Christ's words for us who can invoke his Name as we recall the words spoken to Isaiah: "…even to your old age I am He, and to grey hairs I will carry you. I have made, and I will bear; I will carry and will save." (*Is* 46:4)

The burning bush of the cross

For Pope Benedict XVI, what began at Sinai finds its completion on the cross on Golgotha. In a homily given in Rome on 7th March 2010, Pope Benedict said:

"By revealing his Name, God establishes a relationship between himself and us. He enables us to invoke him, he enters into relations with us and gives us the possibility of being in a relationship with him. This means that he gives himself, in a certain way, to our human world, becoming accessible, as if he were one of us. He faces the risk of the relationship, of being with us. What began in the burning bush in the desert is accomplished in the burning bush of the cross where God, having become accessible in his Son made man, really became one of us, is put into our hands and, in this way, realises the liberation of humanity. On Golgotha God, who during the night of the flight from Egypt revealed himself as the one who frees us from slavery, revealed himself as the one who embraces every human being with the saving power of the cross and the resurrection and liberates him from sin and death, accepts him in the embrace of his love."[9]

For Pope Benedict XVI, the cross is the true burning bush. Men will gaze on the one whom they have pierced and, when Christ has been lifted up on the cross then men will know that he is 'I am'. The meaning of God's name is God's merciful presence among men. If we were to ask what was God's meaning at Sinai and at Golgotha, the answer is that "love was his meaning."

The Name that is Above All Other Names

The *Catechism of the Catholic Church* contains words on the name of Jesus that are breathtaking in their implications:

> "But the one name that contains everything is the one that the Son of God received in his incarnation: JESUS. The divine name may not be spoken by human lips, but by assuming our humanity the Word of God hands it over to us and we can invoke it: 'Jesus', 'YHWH saves'. The name 'Jesus' contains all: God and man and the whole economy of creation and salvation. To pray 'Jesus' is to invoke him and to call him within us. His name is the only one that contains the presence it signifies. Jesus is the Risen One, and whoever invokes the name of Jesus is welcoming the Son of God who loved him and who gave himself up for him." (¶2666)

What strikes us here very forcefully is that the language being used here about the Holy Name of Jesus is sacramental language. The *Catechism* could almost be talking about the Eucharist itself. The name 'Jesus' contains all: the presence of Jesus himself and the whole mystery of salvation. To pray in the name of Jesus is to have access to the Father and it is only by the Holy Spirit that such prayer is possible. For those who call on him in humility of heart, the Name brings into effect what it signifies - the saving presence of Jesus. The name of Jesus is our interface with the Lord himself and here is a way of prayer accessible to all, one that is capable of transforming our spiritual lives.

But why should the name of Jesus contain all and possess such unique power? It is certainly not through any magical property of the Name itself. There is nothing innately mystical in the name itself. To answer this question, we must always keep sharply in focus the fundamental truth that the one who bears the Name, Jesus, the Son of Mary, is both fully God and fully man. Jesus is the name of the Messiah, the name of the Word made flesh.

The hymn in Philippians

The key passage is to be found in St Paul's letter to the Church in Philippi. Probably quoting from a very early Christian hymn, Paul says of Jesus:

> "who, though he was in the form of God, did not count equality with God a thing to be grasped, but emptied

himself, taking the form of a servant, being born in the likeness of men. And being found in human form he humbled himself and became obedient unto death, even death on a cross. Therefore God has highly exalted him and bestowed on him the name which is above every name, that at the name of Jesus every knee should bow, in heaven and on earth and under the earth, and every tongue confess that Jesus Christ is Lord, to the glory of God the Father." (*Ph* 2:6-11)

As a divine person, the Son of God never ceased for one moment to possess the divine nature. He emptied himself by assuming our human nature, not by ceasing to be God. Having been made truly man, Christ came in the likeness of men and appeared among us as all men are. He came not as the King of Kings, surrounded by legions of angels, but entered the world as a tiny Jewish baby who, on the eighth day at his *brit milah*, his circumcision, received the name of Jesus, a name chosen by God himself. He took the form of a bondservant. What was invisible is now visible, what was intangible can now be touched, what was inaudible can now be heard. The Name that could not be spoken by human lips can now be invoked by all.

From the whole flow of the passage, it is evident that the Name that Christ receives cannot simply be the divine title of *Kyrios*, 'Lord', which properly speaking is an attribute rather than a name, or rather the name of a name. In the Greek version of the Old Testament, the Greek *Kyrios* is used to translate the Hebrew YHWH but it is at the name of Jesus that the knee of every creature must bend, and at the name of Jesus that every tongue must confess that Jesus Christ is Lord.

What then is the Name that is above all other names? In Isaiah 45:23, YHWH says: "By myself I have sworn, from my mouth has gone forth in righteousness a word that shall not return: 'To me every knee shall bow, every tongue shall swear.'" (*Is* 45:23) The one who speaks here is the 'I Am', YHWH, who spoke out of the burning bush at the dawn of Israel's redemption. The Name that is above all other names is the four-letter Name of God himself. The one to whom every knee must bend is the Lord.

With this in mind, we begin to see how radical and revolutionary the hymn is. It applies to Jesus words that apply to YHWH himself. What Paul has in mind is the ineffable name of God which is the Name that is above all other names, the Name that denotes God's own inner being, the divine essence itself, He Who Is. As such, this Name is beyond all human speech. But, as is evident from the context and thrust of the words of the hymn, the human name of Jesus is in some transcendent manner united to that mysterious Name. What is said of YHWH and his Name can be said of Jesus and his Name.

After celebrating Christ's perfect obedience even unto death on a cross, the hymn continues in a tone of exultation: it is because of this perfect obedience that God has greatly exalted Christ and bestowed on him the Name that is above every name. The two names are not thereby identical but equivalence of worship is to be given to the name of Jesus. Before the revelation of the Name in time, God knew the name of Jesus from all eternity as the name of the Messiah, the name of Immanuel, God-with-us.

At the name of Jesus

Paul states that it was at the exaltation that God gave Jesus the Name that is above all other names. It is also evident that, for Paul, the divine will expressed in this gift of the Name is precisely that the name of Jesus should receive the same cult as the name of YHWH. But the exaltation is not the giving of divinity to Christ because, as God, Christ is eternally and consubstantially divine. From all eternity, the Son of God is 'He Who Is', and thus the exaltation is the manifestation of what had been hidden from all eternity.

It is because Jesus has received the Name that is above every other name, that at the name of Jesus every tongue must confess that Jesus is Lord. Perhaps Paul's thought can be best understood in the context of what might be termed a Christian *Shema*: "Hear, O Israel: the Lord our God, YHWH and Jesus, the Lord is One."

As we have seen, the whole passage is concerned with the exaltation of the man Jesus, and concludes triumphantly with the statement that Jesus Christ is Lord, to the glory of God the Father. God has given Jesus the Messiah the name that is above all other names in order that "at the name of Jesus every knee should bow... and every tongue confess that Jesus the Messiah is Lord." The giving of the Name is part of the whole process of the exaltation of the sacred humanity of our Lord, a process that necessarily must include the exaltation of the human name of Jesus. The exaltation of the Messiah and the exaltation of the name of the Messiah are inseparably linked.

For Paul, the name of Jesus, the name of the glorified and risen Christ, and the Name that is above all other names, the tetragrammaton, are both one and yet distinct. As Paul says in Colossians 1:15, Christ is "the image of the invisible God, the firstborn of all creation." The name of Jesus is the image of the ineffable Name, just as Jesus is the Image of the Invisible God. We see too a Trinitarian theology in the hymn: the Father gives the Son his Name, the Son who is the one who receives the Name and the Spirit is the one who makes it possible for everyone to declare that Jesus is Lord to the glory of the Father.

In his sacred humanity, from Bethlehem to Calvary, Christ reveals his perfect humility and obedience, culminating in death on the cross. By accepting the shame of death on a cross, he is highly exalted by God and given the name that is above all other names. Having suffered in his sacred humanity, the risen and exalted Christ is to be forever glorified in that humanity. The flesh of Christ is the hinge upon which hangs our salvation. This exaltation of Christ necessarily includes the exaltation of his human name. Just as the humanity of Christ is to be adored because the person who assumed it is a divine person, so the name of Jesus is to be hallowed because it is the name of the One who is Lord: *Kyrios* and *Adonai.*

On the Invocation of the Name

Jesus, I trust in you!

It will come as no surprise that St Faustina should have had a passionate and fervent love for the name of Jesus. In her diary, she wrote:

"January 2, [1937]. The Name of Jesus. Oh, how great is your name, O Lord! It is the strength of my soul. When my strength fails, and darkness invades my soul, your Name is the sun whose rays give light and also warmth, and under their influence the soul becomes more beautiful and radiant, taking its splendour from your Name. When I hear the sweetest name of Jesus, my heartbeat grows stronger, and there are times when, hearing the name of Jesus, I fall into a swoon. My spirit eagerly strains toward Him.

This is a particularly important day for me. On this day I made my first visit connected with the painting of the Image. On this day, the Divine Mercy received special external honour for the first time, although it has been known for a long time, but here it was in the form that the Lord had requested. This day of the sweet name of Jesus reminds me of many special graces."[10]

Recording her famous vision of Christ in her convent cell on 22nd February 1931, she wrote in her diary of Christ's command:

> "Paint an image according to the pattern you see, with the signature: Jesus, I trust in you. I desire that this image be venerated, first in your chapel, and [then] throughout the world. The signature prayer is now said and treasured by millions across the world."[11]

It is a long way in space and in time from the Sinai of Moses to the Poland of Faustina but there is always an inner consistency in God's gracious dealings with man: the name of God means his presence of mercy among us. This simple prayer "Jesus, I trust in you" has been a source of strength and consolation for many millions in times of difficulty and hardship. Through this invocation, we can put our hand into the hand of God and discover that the Blessed One comes to us in the name of the Lord.

There are many ways to use the name of Jesus in prayer. There is great freedom here and a very rich spiritual tradition of devotion to the holy Name. We think of the medieval aspiration "My Jesus, mercy! Mary, help!" or that much loved prayer of Catholic ancestors which was on the lips of the Elizabethan martyr, St Ralph Sherwin, as he went to Tyburn: "Jesus, Jesus, Jesus, be unto me a Jesus."

The Jesus Prayer

For some, simply repeating the name of Jesus with love and attention is enough. As long as the Name is not seen as some form of talisman and there is no attempt to seek after spiritual 'signs and wonders', such a way is, of course, perfectly safe. But the majority tradition of Eastern Christendom is that we should set the name of Jesus in the frame of what has become known as the Jesus Prayer: 'Lord Jesus Christ, Son of God, have mercy on me, a sinner'.

The Name has been given to us so that we may invoke our Lord. The Jesus Prayer is a most marvellous summary of the whole Gospel, a prayer that truly says everything. The first half of the prayer is an act of adoration, a loving acceptance of the whole economy of salvation and of God's tender and merciful love for mankind. We unite our voice with the voice of all creation in proclaiming that 'Jesus is Lord' - *Adonai*, the one who was, who is and is to be, risen and glorious, the King of the Universe and whose kingdom we wish to reign in our hearts. He is 'Jesus', the Lord who is our Saviour and our salvation, and the 'Christ', the longed-for Messiah, the Son of David and the anointed one whose name is like oil poured to heal all our wounds.

Then we affirm that Jesus is the 'Son of God', the eternal and incarnate Word. We are directed to the reciprocal and everlasting flow of love that is the Trinitarian life of God. Through the Son and in the unity of the Spirit, we go to the Father and are drawn ever deeper into the divine life that is the eternal sabbath, the abyss of silence, the source and goal of all.

The second half of the prayer is a plea for mercy, a plea which is not only for forgiveness but for God's gracious self-communication of his own divine life: God is mercy, and to pray for mercy is to pray to partake in that divine life - to be established as sons in the Son. The prayer is our cry for mercy, for salvation from our sins: mercy is God's faithful and compassionate love, the divine pity itself.

Our prayer is grace in return for grace, an expression of our turning back to God, the return home from the long exile; for the gates of repentance are always open, since the Lord our God is rich in mercy. We pray the prayer of the tax collector and, in asking for mercy, we are asking Jesus to be a Jesus unto us, for Jesus is the Mercy of the Father made flesh. To pray for mercy is to pray to share in the divine life itself, for we are sinners who need a Jesus. The prayer concludes with 'me, a sinner', for that is what we are - creatures who need a Jesus.

How to say the Jesus Prayer

The essence of the prayer lies in the fact that it contains the name of Jesus: it is emphatically not some form of Christian mantra but a prayer addressed to a Person from whom the prayer derives its efficacy.

We begin by saying the prayer, quietly, calmly, with trust and perseverance, with sorrow for our sins, with love and with adoration, recognising that no-one can say 'Jesus is Lord' except by the Holy Spirit. At this stage, the prayer is said aloud or silently by the lips. St Paul exhorts us to "pray without ceasing", and we begin with the prayer on our lips, praying it over and over again at all times and places. The beauty of the prayer is its very simplicity: it becomes our constant companion. This is an arduous task for, although described as oral, this stage involves mental prayer, since the mind must be fixed upon the meaning of the words said by the lips, upon the sovereign presence of Jesus and the nothingness and need of man.

If, with God's grace, we persevere, the prayer goes deeper within us, acquiring a rhythm of its own, and gradually our minds become more and more centred on the prayer. The mind finds itself repeating the prayer and it is no longer necessary for it to be said aloud or silently by the lips. Then comes the final stage, the prayer of the heart, when, through the gift of God's transfiguring grace in the Spirit, the prayer enters into our heart, the deep core of our being, as we enter ever more deeply into the presence of him whose Name is our joy and through whom we go to the Father in the transforming gift of the Holy Spirit.

What gives the Jesus Prayer its special power is the fact that it contains this all-powerful Name: the power comes from faith in Jesus, for the prayer does not work mechanically or divorced from the Christian life. Indeed, it presumes the lived normal faithful Christian life and the devout reception of the sacraments. The test of authenticity is, as always, love of our neighbour. The essential thing is to stand consciously in the presence of Jesus, with sorrow for one's sins and in humility of heart, with faith, hope and charity.

At the dawn of Israel's history, God promised that "in every place where I cause my name to be remembered I will come to you and bless you." (*Ex* 20:24). This promise of God is irrevocable as are all his promises. Through baptism, we have become a Temple of God wherein his Name pitches its tent and dwells among us.

The joy of the name

We pray that we may always remember that his Name is in our hearts, asking that he may hallow his Name in us that we in our turn may hallow his name with all our heart, and soul and might. Then we shall discover the blessing of his presence, his faithful kindness and how he has always walked with us on the way even when we knew him not.

When we contemplate the wonders and the glory of the Holy Name, we are like children standing on the beach and looking out with wonder at the vast ocean that stretches out before us. In the name of Jesus, we encounter the ocean of mercy opened up for the whole world, the fount of life, his unfathomable compassion and the boundless joy of his Spirit.

The words of the 'Father of English prose', Richard Rolle, are as true now as they were in the fourteenth century and may fittingly conclude this booklet:

> "If you wish to be on good terms with God, and have his grace direct your life, and come to the joy of love, then fix this name 'Jesus' so firmly in your heart that it never leaves your thought. And when you speak to him using your customary name 'Jesu', in your ear it will be joy, in your mouth honey, and in your heart melody, because it will seem joy to you to hear that name being pronounced, sweetness to speak it, cheer and singing to think it. If you think of the name 'Jesus' continually and cling to it devotedly, then it will cleanse you from sin and set your heart aflame."[12]

Endnotes

[1] *Catechism of the Catholic Church*, ¶204. All quotations from the *Catechism* are taken from the text given on the Vatican website: *http://www.vatican.va/archive/ENG0015/_INDEX.HTM*

[2] Benedict XVI, Pope, *Jesus of Nazareth: The Infancy Narratives*, (London, Bloomsbury, 2012) p. 50

[3] Benedict XVI, Pope, *Jesus of Nazareth: From the Baptism in the Jordan to the Transfiguration* (New York, Doubleday, 2007) p. 143

[4] Ibid., p. 347

[5] Levinas, E., *Beyond the Verse: Talmudic readings and lectures* (Bloomington, Indiana University Press, 1994) p. 121

[6] Josephus, *Antiquities of the Jews, Book II*, 12: 4 *http://www.ccel.org/j/josephus/works/ant-2.htm*

[7] Sacks, J., in *The Authorised Daily Prayer Book of the United Hebrew Congregations of the Commonwealth* (Collins, London, 2006) p. xxxi.

[8] de Leon, L., *The Names of Christ*: translation and introduction by Manuel Duran and William Kluback (Ramsey, New Jersey, 1984) p. 349.

[9] Benedict XVI, Pope, 'Homily for the Third Sunday of Lent', 7th March 2010 *http://www.vatican.va/holy_father/benedict_xvi/homilies/2010/documents/hf_ben-xvi_hom_20100307_parrocchia_en.html*

[10] Kowalska, St Sister M. Faustina, *Diary: Divine Mercy in my soul*, (Stockbridge, Marians of the Immaculate Conception, 1999) p. 339

[11] Ibid., p. 24.

[12] Rolle, R., *The English Writings*, trans. Allen, R.S. (New York, Paulist Press International, 1989) p. 173

Union with God

Living the Christ Life

Fr David Vincent Meconi SJ

St Athanasius famously said that "the Son of God became man so that we might become God". This booklet delves into what it means for a Christian not only to have a relationship with God but become so united with Him that we take part in his divinity.

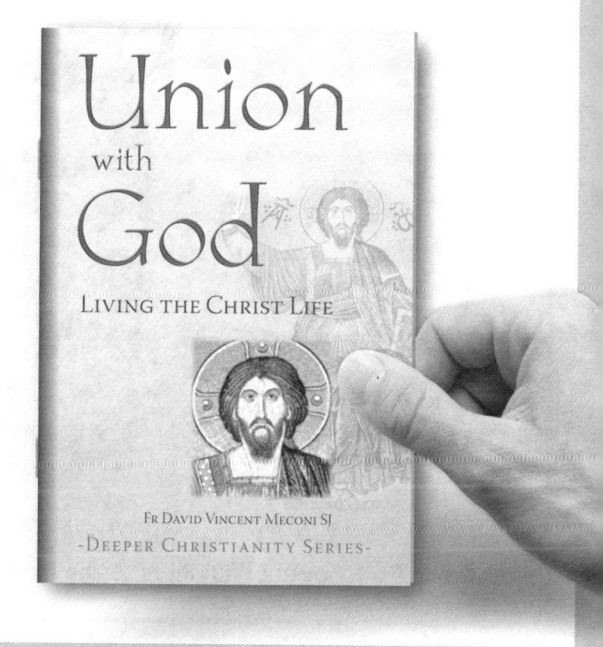

A world of Catholic reading at your fingertips...

Catholic Faith, Life & Truth for all

CTS
www.CTSbooks.org

twitter: @CTSpublishers

facebook.com/CTSpublishers

Catholic Truth Society, Publishers to the Holy See.